Gaming and eSports

HIGH SCORE

THE PEOPLE BEHIND THE GAMES

Kaitlyn Duling

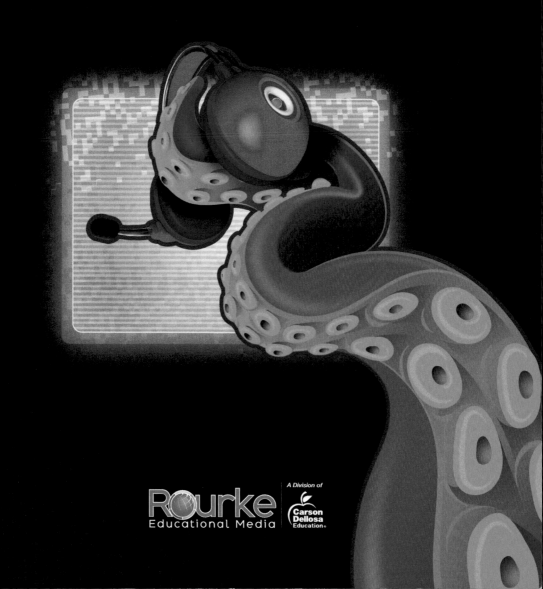

Rourke
Educational Media

A Division of
Carson Dellosa Education

Before Reading: *Building Background Knowledge and Vocabulary*

Building background knowledge can help children process new information and build upon what they already know. Before reading a book, it is important to tap into what children already know about the topic. This will help them develop their vocabulary and increase their reading comprehension.

Questions and Activities to Build Background Knowledge:

1. Look at the front cover of the book and read the title. What do you think this book will be about?
2. What do you already know about this topic?
3. Take a book walk and skim the pages. Look at the table of contents, photographs, captions, and bold words. Did these text features give you any information or predictions about what you will read in this book?

Vocabulary: *Vocabulary Is Key to Reading Comprehension*

Use the following directions to prompt a conversation about each word.

- Read the vocabulary words.
- What comes to mind when you see each word?
- What do you think each word means?

Vocabulary Words:
- code
- developers
- invest
- prize pool
- tournament
- speedrunning
- stream

During Reading: *Reading for Meaning and Understanding*

To achieve deep comprehension of a book, children are encouraged to use close reading strategies. During reading, it is important to have children stop and make connections. These connections result in deeper analysis and understanding of a book.

 Close Reading a Text

During reading, have children stop and talk about the following:

- Any confusing parts
- Any unknown words
- Text to text, text to self, text to world connections
- The main idea in each chapter or heading

Encourage children to use context clues to determine the meaning of any unknown words. These strategies will help children learn to analyze the text more thoroughly as they read.

When you are finished reading this book, turn to the next-to-last page for After-Reading Questions and an Activity.

Table of Contents

Some players win by collecting the most games. Others win by starting eSports teams and making big bucks. Are you ready to meet the people who reach for the top of the leaderboard? Let's get started!

GOING PRO

One of the best things about video games? Anyone can play them. Just pick up a controller and begin! Some people don't play only for fun. Professional gamers take gaming to the next level. A pro gamer is someone who gets paid to play games. They might get paid to practice with a team or to compete in tournaments. They can make even more when they win—a lot more.

Today's top-earning gamers and teams can make millions of dollars, mostly through tournaments. The International, an annual *Dota 2* tournament, boasts the largest **prize pool**. In 2019, there was $34.3 million up for grabs at the International.

Multiplayer Online Battle Arena

NAME GAME

Most pro gamers aren't known by their first and last names. Instead, they go by their gamer names. These are also called tags, handles, or IDs. For example, *Counter-Strike* player Christopher Alesund goes by GeT_RiGhT.

PRIZE POOL (prize pool): the amount of money collected to award as prizes to winning players in a tournament

Prize pools are divided up at tournaments. Each winning team and player receives a portion of the money. Most gamers earn just a few hundred dollars each year, but the top pros earn much, much more than that. DrNykterstein was the top gamer of 2020. He made $510,586.52 playing online speed chess.

Most of the highest-earners play *Dota 2* or *Counter-Strike: Global Offensive*. Players like NOtail, JerA, and MinD_ContRoL have earned millions of dollars throughout their gaming careers.

The cosplayer "rehabGnaked" as "Dota 2" character Ember Spirit at the ESL One Hamburg e-sports event

Pros don't just make money at tournaments. Many pros also **stream** their gameplay. You can watch them play online. Can you imagine millions of people watching you play video games?
A *Fortnite* player called Ninja streams his games to over 12 million followers.

Some pro gamers don't just play together—they live together! Gaming houses gather players in one place to train and stream. Cloud9, 100 Thieves, and Team Queso are three well-known gaming houses.

STREAM (streem):
to broadcast gameplay via the internet so that other people can watch on their computers, phones, or consoles

FAMOUS GAMERS

The gaming world has its own celebrities. eSports athletes like Faker and MATUMBMAN are well-known in gaming circles. While some people are famous for gaming, some are famous and just happen to play games!

Today, video games have gone mainstream. Actor Zac Efron loves to play Halo. Actress Mila Kunis is wild about *World of Warcraft* and *Call of Duty*. United States Representative Alexandria Ocasio-Cortez has streamed herself playing *Among Us*! In some ways, celebrities are just like us.

GAMES ⌄   SHOP ⌄

ZARD

WORLD
of
WARCRAFT
15 YEAR ANNIVERSARY

Mila Kunis

13

Some celebrities take their love for video games a step further. Actress Kristen Bell lends her voice to three *Assassin's Creed* games. Singer Jesse McCartney's voice can be heard on the radio in the *Kingdom Hearts* games. Actor Elijah Wood lent his voice to one of the most famous video game characters of all time—Spyro! You can hear Wood's voice in the *Legend of Spyro* trilogy.

Look closely while you're playing, and you might spot some celebrities in your games. Singers Marshmello, Taylor Swift, and Run the Jewels have all appeared in video games. Games like *Madden*, *FIFA*, and *NBA LIVE* feature real-life players.

WHAT'S THAT SOUND?

If you've played video games, you may have heard Steve Blum's voice. His voice has been featured in more games than any other voice actor. His voice can be heard in *Dota 2*, *Final Fantasy XV*, *Batman: Arkham Knight*... and more than 360 other games!

Elijah Woods

Kristen Bell

Steve Blum

Jack Black voiced Eddie Riggs in
Brütal Legend and maintains a
video game streaming presence on
his YouTube channel JablinskiGames.

Over the past few years, some celebrities have found a new way to get involved in video gaming. They have started to **invest** in eSports. They are buying teams, funding gaming organizations, and betting big on gaming. Athletes such as Shaq, Michael Jordan, and Steph Curry have invested money in eSports. Even Ashton Kutcher and Jennifer Lopez have added their money to the mix.

Celebrities who invest in eSports expect to get a big payout. They believe that eSports will only grow more popular in the years ahead. They could be right! Only time will tell.

INVEST (in-VEST):
to give or lend money to something with the intention of getting more money back later

Shaq

Michael Jordan

Steph Curry

KAZAAAM!

Some of the legendary "players" in video gaming don't use a controller. Instead, they develop and design the games. Shigeru Miyamoto is one of the most prolific game **developers** out there. Some call him the "Walt Disney of video games."

Since joining Nintendo in 1981, Miyamoto has designed and worked on hundreds of games. *Donkey Kong, Mario*, *Pikmin*, and *The Legend of Zelda* are just a few of his creations.

Shigeru Miyamoto

A FAN FAVORITE

Do you have a favorite video
game character? Twitter users
have voted with their clicks.
With 5.8 million followers,
Sonic the Hedgehog is the most-
followed video game character
on Twitter!

19

Most eSports athletes play their games just as you would at home. But a growing number of athletes excel at a specific type of gameplay called **speedrunning**. In speedruns, players try to play through full games as quickly as possible.

On Twitch and YouTube, you can watch speedruns of games like *Pokémon Red*, *Super Mario 64*, and *Portal*. A player named Zudu holds the world record for beating *The Legend of Zelda: Ocarina of Time* in under 8 minutes! The player zooms through by using glitches in the game's **code**.

SPEEDRUNNING (speed ruhn-ing):
completing a video game, or level of a game, as fast as possible

CODE (kode):
computer language instructions that control every aspect of a game, allowing it to operate

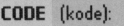

When it comes to video games, there's always room for improvement. Gamers can play faster, play smarter, and beat games in new ways. With thousands of pro gamers and dozens of high-level events each year, new eSports champions are crowned almost every day. Some of the biggest events invite players to compete in *Overwatch*, *Hearthstone, Counter-Strike: Global Offensive, Call of Duty*, and *League of Legends*.

The newest games may attract top pros, but the eSports world makes room for vintage games too. The Classic Tetris World Championship brings contestants together to play the 1989 version of the game. They play on the original Nintendo Entertainment System (NES) console.

Classic Tetris World Championship

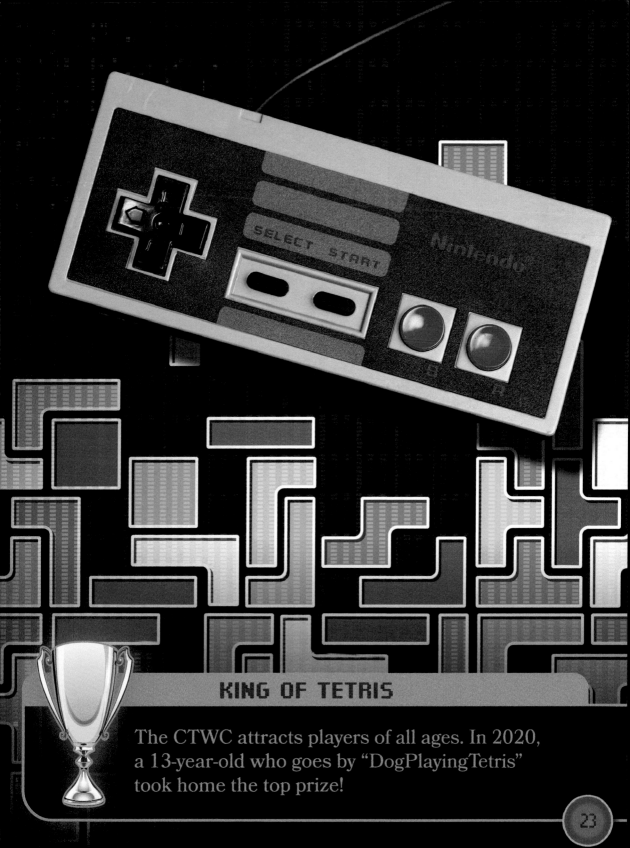

KING OF TETRIS

The CTWC attracts players of all ages. In 2020, a 13-year-old who goes by "DogPlayingTetris" took home the top prize!

FOR THE LOVE OF THE GAME

Do you love video games? Do you really, really love video games? You're not alone! Across the globe, there are about 2.7 billion gamers. In fact, 75 percent of all U.S. households have at least one person who plays video games. A full 70 percent of people under the age of 18 play video games. That's a lot of gaming!

A DIFFERENT KIND OF SPEEDRUN

Video gamers have all sorts of hobbies, and this world record proves it! In 2016, John Kelly set the record for running the fastest marathon while dressed as a video game character. Kelly ran 26.2 miles in under three hours—all while dressed as Link from *The Legend of Zelda*.

Many gamers dream of going pro one day. For some, the first step to making money with gaming is a college scholarship. To secure scholarships, students must practice their games in middle and high school. Today, high schools in more than 17 states offer eSports teams. Middle schools and grade schools are starting to form teams too. The earlier they start playing competitively, the more likely it is that students will get scholarships, putting their dreams of pro gaming careers within reach.

LIVING THE DREAM

With 20,139 video games, Antônio Monteiro has the largest video game collection in the world. Luckily, he also has more than a hundred consoles. That means he can play all day, every day, forever!

We might think of gaming as an activity for young people, but gamers of all ages love to plug in and play. The Silver Snipers team of Stockholm, Sweden, is made up of players over the age of 60. They are a pro team that plays *Counter-Strike* at tournaments across Europe. The back of their jackets reads, "We've got time to kill."

On the other end of the spectrum is the youngest pro gamer. Victor De Leon III, gamer tag Lil Poison, signed his first pro deal at the age of seven. He attended his first *Halo* tournament at just four years old. When it comes to video games, age has *nothing* to do with how high you can score. With practice and passion, anyone can become a video game champion.

Bungie's Master Chief
from the Halo series

MEMORY GAME

Look at the pictures. What do you remember
reading on the pages where each image appeared?

INDEX

AFTER-READING QUESTIONS

1. Why do you think people pursue careers in eSports?

2. What are three different ways to become a champion in the video game world?

3. How do people earn money in eSports?

4. Why would a young gamer join a school eSports team?

5. What are some of the biggest games in professional eSports?

ACTIVITY

Do you dream of becoming a video game champion? Start today! Create your own video game name. Then draw the team uniform you will wear, and come up with a team name. Be as creative as you'd like. It's your name and your team! Someday, it might be your big win.

ABOUT THE AUTHOR

Kaitlyn Duling is a lifelong lover of video games. She enjoys games that get her moving, thinking, and dreaming. When she's not on her Nintendo Switch, Kaitlyn is writing and living in Washington, DC. She has authored over 100 books for kids and teens.

www.rourkeeducationalmedia.com

PHOTO CREDITS ©: cover: FRED PROUSER/REUTERS/Newscom; page 3: Inked Pixels/Shutterstock.com; page 4: imageBROKER/Moritz Wolf/Newscom; page 5: MicroOne/ Shutterstock.com; page 6: JASON REDMOND/REUTERS/Newscom; page 8: Imagine China/Newscom; page 9: Daniel Reinhardt/dpa/picture-alliance/Newscom; page 10: Dean Drobot/ Shutterstock.com; page 12: Choudhary/ Shutterstock.com; page 13: ll.studio/Shutterstock.com; page 13: Tinseltown/ Shutterstock.com; page 15: s_bukley/ Shutterstock.com; page 15: Tinseltown/ Shutterstock.com; page 15: Featureflash Photo Agency/ Shutterstock.com; page 15: Kathy Hutchins/ Shutterstock.com; page 17: Birdie Thompson/AdMedia/SIPA/Newscom; page 17: Ron Adar/ Shutterstock.com; page 17: landmarkmedia/ Shutterstock.com; page 18: JUAN CARLOS ROJAS/NOTIMEX/Newscom; page 19: rafapress/ Shutterstock.com; page 19: Nicescene/ Shutterstock.com; page 19: Wachiwit/ Shutterstock.com; page 21: Mantav Jivva/ Shutterstock.com; page 21: seeshooteatrepeat/ Shutterstock.com; page 21: Roman Kosolapov/ Shutterstock.com; page 23: Peter Gudella/ Shutterstock.com; page 23: Bobnevv/ Shutterstock.com; page 23: AlexVector/ Shutterstock.com; page 23: Pixel Embargo/ Shutterstock.com; page 24: robtek/ Shutterstock.com; page 27: Imagine China/Newscom; page 27: Roman Kosolapov/ Shutterstock.com; page 29: Stuart Isett/Polaris/Newscom; page 29: ANNEGRET HILSE/REUTERS/Newscom; page 29: OHishiapply/ Shutterstock.com; n/a: amtitus/ Getty Images

Edited by: Jennifer Doyle
Cover design and illustration by: Joshua Janes
Interior design and illustrations by: Joshua Janes

Library of Congress PCN Data

High Score The People Behind The Games / Kaitlyn Duling
(Gaming and eSports)
ISBN 978-1-73164-932-4 (hard cover)
ISBN 978-1-73164-880-8 (soft cover)
ISBN 978-1-73164-984-3 (e-Book)
ISBN 978-1-73165-088-7 (e-Pub)
Library of Congress Control Number: 2021935269

Rourke Educational Media
Printed in the United States of America
02-3082211938